J.S. BACH

TWO-PART INVENTIONS
THE LEFT HAND ON BASS GUITAR

J. S. Bach - Two-Part Inventions: The Left Hand on Bass Guitar

Copyright © 2022 by Bosco Brothers Ltd.

First Printing 2022

ISBN: 978-1-7399795-2-2

For comments, queries, or corrections, please visit:
www.boscobrothers.com

BOSCO BROTHERS

J. S. BACH

Two-Part Inventions

THE LEFT HAND ON BASS GUITAR

INTRODUCTION

Each of the two-voiced Inventions is included with the original keyboard grand staff, showing the left- and right-hand voices. The tablature is the left-hand transcribed an octave down for bass guitar.

Due to the limited range of the standard 4-string bass guitar, some single notes and even some phrases have been transposed up an octave. These are marked with an asterisk (*), and most of them can be played in the correct octave with a 5-string bass with a low B.

The fingerings laid out in this book are but one of many options and are a good mixture between ease of play and maintaining a consistent timbre. To this end, open strings have been avoided unless the alternative is unnecessarily hard to play. For trickier parts, exact finger numbers have been indicated above the tablature. The reader is encouraged to experiment with alternative fingerings.

Pay attention to the legato phrases in the keyboard notation. With fretted instruments, the modern use of legato usually means *hammer-ons* and *pull-offs*. However, for classical keyboard music, the legato phrases should simply be played smoothly and connected.

Bach did not include any tempo or volume markings in his Inventions. Many of them lend themselves, however, to either a slower or faster tempo.

Of course, the Inventions contain two voices that are designed to work together. Nevertheless, there is enough material contained within a single voice from which one can profit. Finding a colleague (perhaps a guitarist) to play the first voice will be a shared delight.

This book can be seen as an entry point to the Inventions. A wealth of information can be obtained by carefully analysing, researching, learning, practising and playing these short masterpieces. Bass guitar students from any level and style will be richly rewarded for their efforts.

ORNAMENTS

To authentically realise the music from the Baroque period, it is necessary to interpret the various ornaments as Bach intended. The following key is adapted directly from Bach's own hand-written "Explication" from his *Klavierbüchlein*. Bach's original names are included alongside their closest modern English equivalents in parenthesis ("Idem" means "the same name as the previous one").

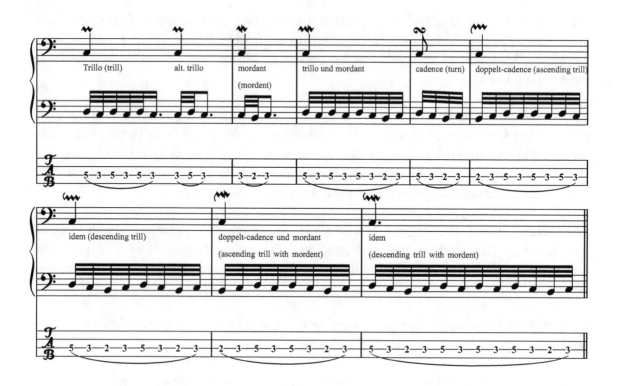

For fretted instruments, these can all be played with *hammer-ons* and *pull-offs*.

In his "Explication", Bach shows the ornaments applied only to quarter and eighth notes, so it serves only as a general indication of their function. At moderate tempos, *trill*s are much shorter. *Trill*s should begin on the upper note and be a minimum of four notes. All ornaments begin *on* the beat and remain diatonic to the current key.

The "alt. trillo" is often shown in non-contemporary publications, which may be more suitable for bass guitar.

Ornaments are a matter of taste and listening to popular recordings can shed some light on this expansive topic. Glenn Gould is recommended.

Ornaments are *embellishments* and, if the player wishes, can (but should not) be omitted entirely. The short *trill* and *mordent* are the most common and characteristic of the era and so perhaps the most necessary to keep.

INVENTIONS

Invention 1 (in C Major)

BWV 772

Invention 2 (in C Minor)

BWV 773

Invention 3 (in D Major)

BWV 774

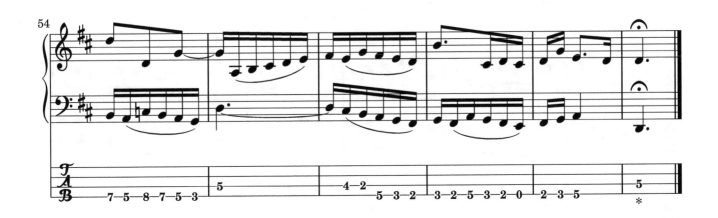

Invention 4 (in D Minor)

BWV 775

Invention 5 (in E♭ Major)

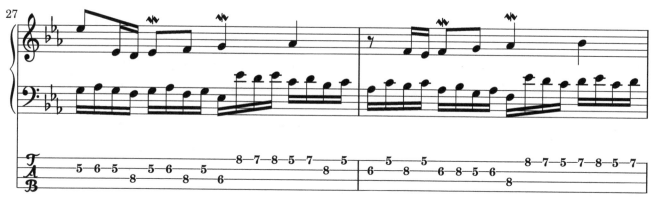

Invention 6 (in E Major)

BWV 777

Invention 7 (in E Minor)

BWV 778

Invention 8 (in F Major)

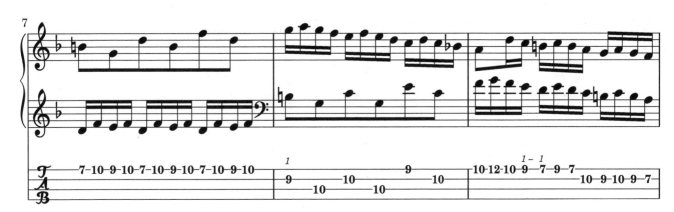

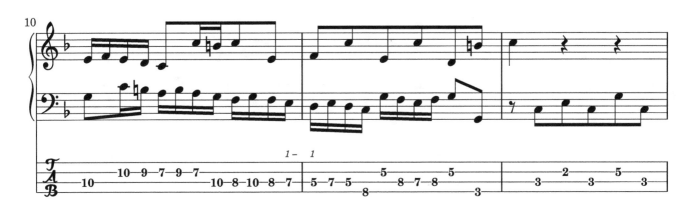

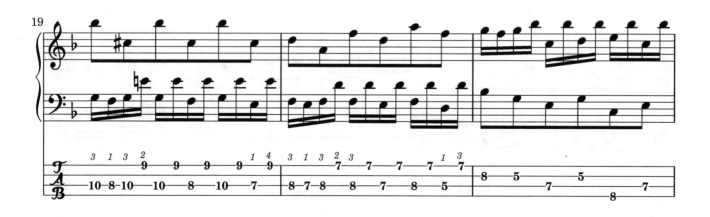

Invention 9 (in F Minor)

BWV 780

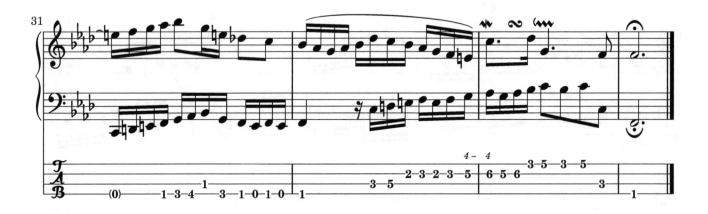

Invention 10 (in G Major)

BWV 781

Invention 11 (in G Minor)

BWV 782

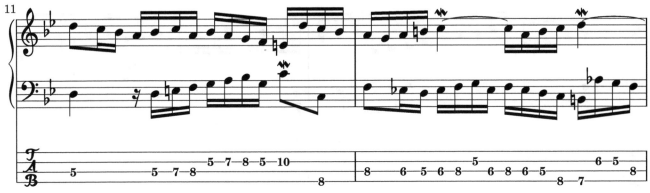

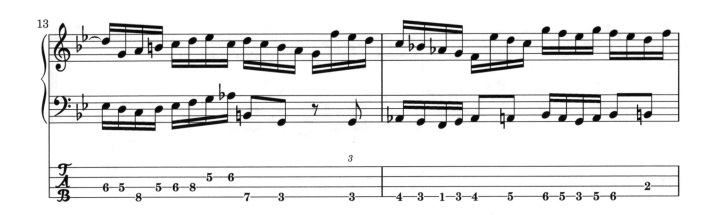

Invention 12 (in A Major)

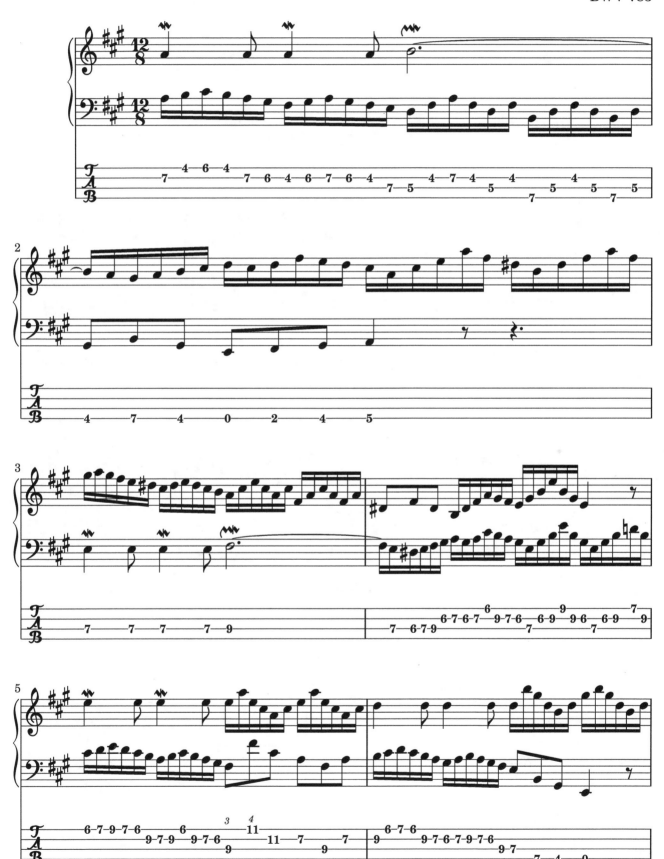

Invention 13 (in A Minor)

BWV 784

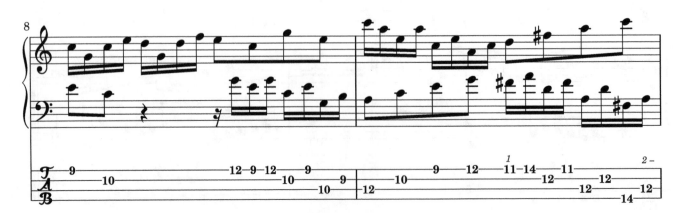

Invention 14 (in B♭ Major)

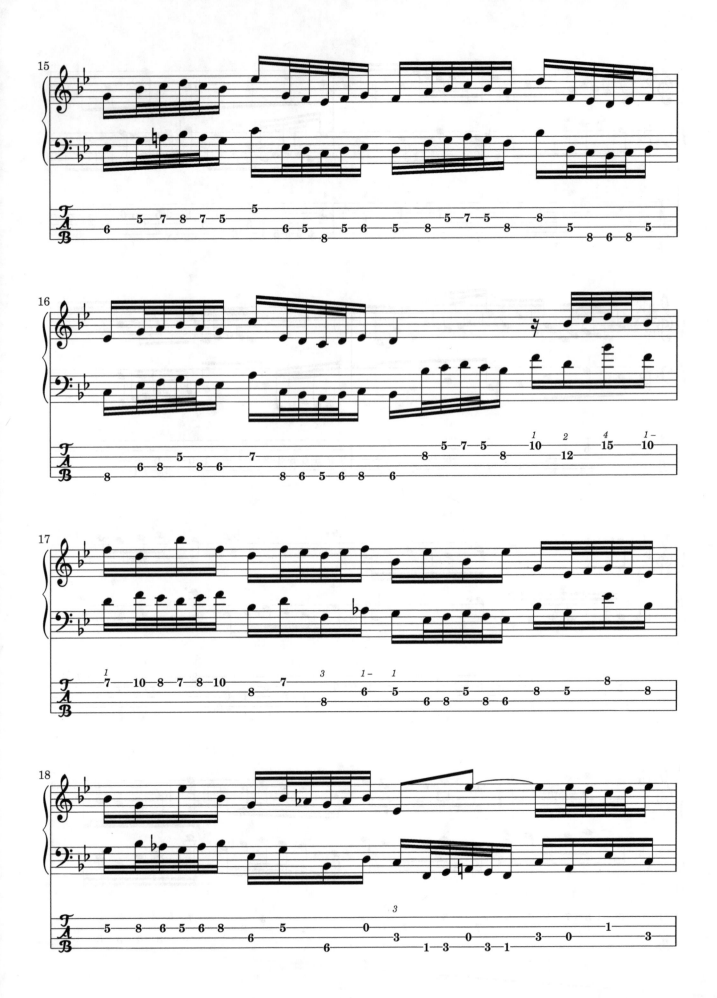

Invention 15 (in B Minor)

BWV 786

Printed in the USA
CPSIA information can be obtained
at www.ICGtesting.com
LVHW071053141223
766408LV00009B/724